I0468602

GAMIFICATION

The Industry's Biggest Secrets Revealed

By
Tom Raycove
For
Disrupted Logic's ctalyst™
www.disruptedlogic.com

Disrupted Logic Interactive Inc.
Suite 210 8120 128th Street
Surrey, BC V3W 1R1
www.disruptedlogic.com

Note about images and logos:

Table of Contents

Introduction 4

Who is This Book For? 6

Why is Gamification Important? 6

Some Basic Terminology 7

What Are Games? 9

What is Gamification? 11

What Gamification is Not 14

Gamification in Business, Marketing, Advertising, Retail and Games 16

    Application in Business 17

    Application in Marketing and Advertising 17

    Application in Retail 18

    Application in Games 18

Using Gamification to Influence Behavior 19

Human Behavior 20

    Cognitive Dissonance 20

    Psychological Factors 23

    Hierarchy of Human Needs 23

Reinforcers 25

Motivators 27

    Extrinsic Motivators 29

    Intrinsic Motivators 31

        Community 34

        Meaning 36

        Mastery 39

        Autonomy 45

    Rules and Boundaries for Rewards 48

    Story (Intrinsic Motivator) 49

    Motivation Driving the Audience 52

    I Expect and Want to Fail 52

    Engagement 54

    Techniques to Permanent Engagement 54

    Abandonment (Avoiding It) 55

Gamification Mechanics 56

Motivational Behaviors, Mechanics 56
and Devices.. 56
From Activity to Engagement 61
Fun 62
   Problem Solving 62
   Collaboration.. 62
   Exploration.. 63
   Building... 63

Rewards 63
Real-World Benefits versus Virtual 64
(In-Game) Benefits... 64
Rewards for The Sake of Rewards............................ 65
Value of The Rewards 66
Rewards Frequency... 67
   Secrets to Success 70
Reward Elements and Mechanics 70
Using Negative Motivators 75

Applying Concepts and Making a Gamification Plan 76
Understanding Your Objectives............................... 76
Build Engagement... 77
Putting The Plan to Work 79

3 Examples of Gamification Used in Marketing 81
Starbucks My Rewards...................................... 81
Heineken Star Player 82
M&M's Eye-Spy Pretzel.................................... 82

3 Examples of Gamification Used in Business 83
Giff Gaff Magical Gamification 83
BlueWolf 83
The US Army 84

Facilities, Providers and Resources 85

Introduction

Hey...thank you for purchasing our book on Gamification. We gratefully appreciate it and every bit of support goes a long way towards helping build a stronger and more engaged community.

Gamification is a term that was first coined by Nick Pelling in 2002. However, the practice and use of Gamification concepts is older than you might think.

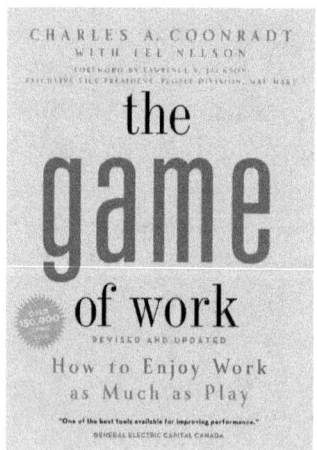

In 1973, Charles Coonradt wrote a book titled *"The Game of Work: How to Enjoy Work as Much as Play"*.

In his book, Charles reveals what motivates and inspires people to excel in sports and recreational activities and then applies these concepts to business leadership methods.

He looked at many daily business challenges like employee satisfaction, motivation and bottom-line profitability, and how they can be improved using simple sports and recreational motivators.

You can find the most recent edition of Charles Coonradt's published book on Amazon here:

http://www.amazon.com/Game-Work-Charles-Coonradt/dp/1423630858

Since then, the concept of Gamification and its use in business, marketing, advertising and video games *(in particular mobile video games)* has gained huge momentum. It's become so essential in mobile development, that it is often the single biggest influencer of success or failure.

The founders of ctalyst™ have over 30 years of experience in video games, movies, television, sports, marketing, advertising and business.

Our projects have been seen around the world and played by hundreds of millions of people.

We help people just like you turn their content in to money making properties. Stop by and check out our website at http://www.disruptedlogic.com

This book was made because it's difficult to find one simple, complete and easy to understand resource that gives a great explanation of what Gamification is, all while guiding you through the process of making your own road map and help you to apply Gamification to your own projects.

We hope that you'll find this book informative, simple and of great value as you move forward with your marketing, advertising, business, apps and games projects.

We're always looking for ways that we can be of help to you. We are always open to any suggestions, tips or even advice on how we can improve and be of better help.

Who is This Book For?

Anyone who is busy running a business, retail store, advertising or marketing agency or manages advertising or marketing campaigns, or runs and manages a development company, website, blog and needs to inspire, motivate and engage an audience will find this book handy.

This book has been written for anyone who doesn't have a lot of time but really needs some great, solid information right away.

Why is Gamification Important?

Gamification has become one of the most important and powerful methods of motivating and inspiring people's behaviors.

It can be used to differentiate one company from another, create and generate loyalty to products, brands, and brand messages, and to increase the stickiness of a brand or its products with an audience.

Gamification greatly increases the frequency and volume of consumer engagement by presenting activities that are exciting, interesting and fun and over a longer period of time. Consumers engage longer and far more often when presented with a gamification approach.

It all comes down to motivating people to take the actions you want. When you make it fun, interesting, easy and rewarding, people are much more inclined to continue and to react the way you want them to.

Gamification increases engagement, competition, progression and contributes to a habit forming environment.

Some Basic Terminology

Image Lincense Creative Commons:
https://creativecommons.org/licenses/by/2.0/
Author: www.flickr.com/photos/stf-o

Games and the game concepts of game development may be foreign or new to you. We're going to be making using of certain industry terminology in this book.

Instead of making you flip to the back of the book or jump online, let's get started right now with a few of the basics.

Game Mechanics:

All games are built from various systems of mechanics. Mechanics are all of the rules, boundaries and methods the developers or designers use to get you to interact and play. These can include pretty much anything you can think of that end up forming the game. In short, game mechanics are what makes the game a game and what makes the game successful.

Game Elements:

The term Game Elements is rather vague and yet all inclusive. It's real meaning comes from the context of how the term is actually being used. Game elements can include objects, characters, environments, tools, rules, graphics, feedback, interactions, competition, goals, social binders and much more. Think of game elements as the various bits, pieces and even Game Mechanics that make up a particular game.

Game Design:

Our friends at Wikipedia (https://en.wikipedia.org/wiki/Game_design) define Game Design as the art of applying design and aesthetics to create a game to facilitate interaction between players for entertainment purposes. Game design can be applied both to games and to other interactions.
That's an awful lot of words to simply say that Game Design is the look, structure, feel and play that makes a game so much fun and super cool.

Game Theory:

Game theory is the study and application of decision making processes where players and participants must make choices that affect the outcome of the game and the effect of choices and decisions on the interests of other players and participants. The concepts of game theory help to define and describe the structure and strategic scenarios of gaming by explaining why people make certain choices and how those choices impact others.

Game Dynamics:

Game Dynamics play off the human psyche by creating desirable feedback loops that serve to lead people to learn more, improve their skills and increase their accomplishments.

Or simply put, Game Dynamics are the interactive and engaging bits.

Users, Gamers, Audience, Consumers, Customers or Participants:

We'll be using the terms Users, Gamers, Audience, Consumers, Customers and or Participants throughout the book. The terms are being used interchangeably and are meant to represent the people you are targeting with your Gamification plan.

What Are Games?

In a nutshell, games are simply any form of play for the sake of fun and entertainment.

But first, here's how Wikipedia defines games (https://en.wikipedia.org/wiki/Game):

> *"...a game is structured form of play, usually undertaken for enjoyment and sometimes used as an educational tool. Games are distinct from work, which is usually carried out for remuneration, and from art, which is more often an expression of aesthetic or ideological elements. However, the distinction is not clear-cut, and many games are also considered to be work (such as professional players of spectator sports or games) or art (such as jigsaw puzzles or games involving an artistic layout such as Mahjong, solitaire, or some video games).*
>
> *Key components of games are goals, rules, challenge, and interaction. Games generally involve mental or physical stimulation, and often both. Many games help develop practical skills, serve as a form of exercise, or otherwise perform an educational, simulational, or psychological role.*
>
> *Attested as early as 2600 BC, games are a universal part of human experience and present in all cultures.*

The Royal Game of Ur, Senet, and Mancala are some of the oldest known games."

Phew! That's quite a mouth full and I'm sure it just shot our Flesch-Kincaid readability score through the roof.

It's easy enough to summarize in more simple terms. There are five basic aspects that we can use to help see if a task is actually a game:

Voluntary:

Is it voluntary? The choice of playing a game must be entirely voluntary. Gamers, players, your audience...they must have the option to play or not. If it's not optional, it's not a game.

Fun:

Is it supposed to be fun? It has to be fun and for the purpose of entertainment. If it's not fun, if it's not entertaining, it's a chore.

Goals:

Are there goals? Games have at least one major goal (winning) and optionally many smaller goals. The successful completion of a goal leads to some form of a reward.

Rules:

Are there rules or boundaries? Rules are the laws that explain the heart of the playful experience. They serve to guide players through mastery of each goal.

Feedback:

And finally, games must have some form of feedback that lets the players see and understand the meaning of their achievements as they move along within the experience.

If you really want to dig deep on want makes a game, well … a game, there are many University and College courses on the subject. Instead, let's stick with the simple basics.

A game is:

- Voluntary
- Fun
- Goal focused
- Rule based
- Feedback driven

What is Gamification?

Gamification is about making non-game tasks, activities and events fun.

Gamification is about influencing and encouraging desired behaviors. It's about giving useful and faster feedback along with reasons to engage and quantified motivation.

Gamification gives context and meaning to the decision making process, provides feedback that helps track progress and gives measurable goals to achievements.

Video game developers discovered something years ago that most businesses are just now figuring out:

> *Gamers are extremely motivated, highly disciplined and fast learners. And when it comes to repetitive tasks, gamers have a never ending supply of energy and focus.*

The idea of Gamification as we know it today comes from the development of popular video games.

But interestingly enough, Gamification isn't a term that's common in the game industry.

The concept and idea of Gamification applies mostly non-game activities and processes. It's used to encourage and influence people by engaging them more with technology, encouraging desired behaviors, solving problems and allowing for mastery and autonomy without distraction.

Over the past years, marketers, advertisers and business people who are not connected with the gaming industry have begun to ask how they can make Gamification work for them. How they can leverage the enjoyment, engagement and benefits of games to motivate and inspire their customers to take desired actions.

Savvy marketers have learned there are key elements related to the gaming industry that can be used to convert leads to prospects, and prospects to customers.

Gamification makes use of game elements, game theory and game mechanics and design to inspire and encourage the interaction and engagement of a consumer in return for rewards.

> It's a technique that takes advantage of our built-in DNA to play and win games.

People are naturally and intuitively hardwired to achieve goals. Gamification plays off our desire to compete, achieve, gain status, autonomy and validation within our social groups.

We can use common gaming concepts like point scoring, leader-boarding, progress and progress feedback, achievements, levels and leveling, badges, rewards and other familiar devices, to encourage our audience to interact and engage with the experience we're presenting.

By making regular every-day activities fun, entertaining and rewarding we can influence and guide their behaviors. Gamification naturally comes from the world of games, but it fits incredibly well when applied to any of a number of non-game activities and events.

By making a task fun, identifying a set of goals, defining rules and boundaries, providing feedback and rewards, and providing a sense of community and social acceptance and validation, your audience will continuously take the actions you have designed for them.

The real, practical and down to Earth goal of Gamification is to engage the audience so that you can influence and reward their behaviors through activities they believe are fun.

What Gamification is Not

First, let's just make one thing clear: **Gamification has little to do with the video game industry!**

It's not about sneaking games in to your marketing or advertising, it's not about reaching the gaming demographic and it's definitely not about becoming a game developer to promote your business.

While a video game is created solely to give the gamer a great time, Gamification includes fun combined with specific goal purposes that are linked to non-game related activities like marketing, advertising, retail or business.

Many marketers, advertisers and business people mistakenly believe that Gamification is just gaming in disguise. They believe it's a thinly veiled attempt to distract leads, prospects and consumers from the *pitch*.

The reality couldn't be further from the truth. Gamification is about making the pitch fun, enjoyable, interactive and engaging. It's about capturing the interests, hearts, minds and souls of your prospects and leads. It's about turning prospects and leads into raving fans!

Mad Men

Television shows gain audience by advertising. The advertising tends to be boring, typical and predictable.

Every show follows the same format and uses the same old, tired techniques.

The television show "*Mad Men*" changed all of that. Mad Men used Gamification to create massive viral buzz … and it worked like a charm!

Their unique campaign was titled "Mad Men Yourself" and allowed fans of the show to create stylized 1960's avatars of themselves and share their avatars after connecting their social networks. The end result was over half a million visitors to their website within the first week along with record viewing audiences and ratings.

Old Spice

How hard is it to market a commercial?

I can't imagine anything more difficult. But Old Spice nailed it in spades with an incredibly basic Gamification principle: autonomy and feedback.

"The Man Your Man Could Smell Like" was a brilliant piece of advertising genius that will go down in the ledgers of history as the best ever.

But then Old Spice cranked up a notch again by taking their brilliance to the social world with "Old Spice Man Responds".

They uploaded over 180 videos to YouTube and then

made video responses to comments using the same wit featured in the commercials. The end results were millions upon millions of impressions and views.

Ace Hardware

Ace Hardware set out to attract a younger, more affluent client in order to compete directly against big box retailers.

Independent dealers across America used a Gamified mobile strategy that offered their customers access to unique and new mobile loyalty programs, coupons and high-value bonus offers. The Gamified experience was designed to move people in to brick-and-mortar stores.

The end result was a 300% increase in post-engagement, 26.5% CTR and over a 100% increase in the in-store cart sizes at checkout.

*The **only** connection Gamification has to game development is "fun." Games are fun and Gamification is about making experiences fun with the purpose of manipulating behaviors and actions for alternative reasons.*

Gamification in Business, Marketing, Advertising, Retail and Games

Gamification techniques can be easily applied to Business, Marketing, Advertising, Retail and yes...Games, to massively increase user and consumer engagement.

Companies, developers and marketers who have used Gamification techniques have seen overnight improvements in their conversions from as little as 6-7 times and as much as 70-80 times!

With ctalyst™ (http://www.disruptedlogic.com or http://www.ctalyst.com), we saw a CTR improvement of 555 times Google AdWords' and over 4,300 times the Facebook Ad Network.

Application in Business

When applied the right way, your business can use the concept of Gamification to motivate staff, develop skills, solve problems, improve employee performance, change and correct behaviors, encourage positive internal competition, create brand awareness and encourage customer loyalty.

Application in Marketing and Advertising

Loyalty programs, air miles and frequency programs are examples of how marketers use Gamification to create more business with their leads and prospects. By providing immediate feedback, marketers and advertisers appeal to a built-in human psychological need.

Game scores become business goals and marketers win. Gamification gives marketers and advertisers big opportunities to socially and virally engage their audiences.

It's more about improving the experience than it is about selling and pitching products.

Application in Retail

Gamification makes it really easy for retailers to create engagement strategies that are fun and rewarding.

Mapping, micro-targeting, micro-targeting within the store itself, contests, frequent rewards and loyal customer rewards all help create an environment in which customers enjoy their experience with the retailer.

A simple coupon or special discount is no longer enough to drive traffic through doors. There's too much competition and customers can easily make other choices. Instead, retailers who use Gamification are able to strengthen their relationships with their customers by making brand interactions and purchases a lot more fun and engaging.

A great example are tiered rewards programs that offer a range of new benefits as the customer passes through a series of targeted shopping milestones.

Application in Games

Gamification within games is a natural fit. However, a great many game developers either completely overlook the benefits of Gamification, are not aware, or completely miss the opportunities.

The competition for game playing audiences is intense. There are over 500,000 games on iTunes and Google Play.

It's not enough to make a game that is "fun" to play.

Games now have to be fiercely engaging and need to carefully apply all Gamification techniques to get noticed and survive.

Gamification in games is the difference between massive success and heartbreaking failure.

Using Gamification to Influence Behavior

Just in case you're not familiar with Pavolov's dogs, the basic story goes like this:

> Ivan Petrovich Pavlov (https://en.wikipedia.org/wiki/Ivan_Pavolv), was not just an old-timey dude sporting the manliest beard you've ever seen, he was also a physiologist specializing in the science of conditioning.
>
> He's most famous for an experiment where he conditioned his dogs by ringing a bell at every meal time. After a while, the dogs would salivate each time the bell was rung, regardless of whether dinner was being served.
>
> This experiment eventually led to a greater understanding of how human behaviors work. Questions like what motivates us, what triggers cause reactions and more gave birth to modern Motivational Psychology.

To truly understand how you can apply Gamification strategies to your business, marketing, advertising or apps and games, you'll need a small understanding of *Motivational Psychology*.

Don't worry, we're going to keep it simple and easy.

Human Behavior

Wikipedia (https://en.wikipedia.org/wiki/Human_behavior) defines Human Behavior as the array of every physical action and observable emotion associated with individuals, as well as the human race as a whole. While specific traits of one's personality and temperament may be more consistent, other behaviors will change as one moves from birth through adulthood.

Here's the simple definition: *human behavior is the study of what people do, how they do it and how their behaviors change over time.*

Cognitive Dissonance

Cognitive Dissonance is an interesting psychological concept. It's an important one to understand if you want your Gamification plan to work.

Rewarding behaviors, creating engagements and motivating behaviors can be a delicate balancing act.

By accidentally challenging the *perceived value* of a goal by over or under rewarding the behavior that leads to accomplishing the goal, can result in *disengagement*.

Cognitive Dissonance is the mental stress or discomfort experienced by an individual who holds two or more contradictory beliefs, ideas, or values at the same time, performs an action that is contradictory to one or more beliefs, ideas or values, or is confronted by new information that conflicts with existing beliefs, ideas or values.
(Wikipedia: https://en.wikipedia.org/wiki/Cognitive_dissonance)

Think of Cognitive Dissonance as challenging someone's attitudes or beliefs. The challenge causes mental discomfort and the only way to get relief is to restore a sense of balance. Sometimes this means altering the belief.

Imagine a door you need to pass through and the sign say both Push and Pull. Which do you choose to believe? Regardless of your choice, your beliefs will be challenge.

Our belief in what the goal is truly worth can be easily and accidentally challenged by the reward offered for it. If the reward is greater, the perceived value of the goal is reduced. If the reward is less, the perceived value of the goal increases.

The economic crash of 2008 caused business owners to panic. Many businesses chose to deeply reduce the price of highly valued products or services, sometimes at a major loss just to keep their customers.

The result was a general perception that the original value of the product or service was false to begin with. The sense of the original became greatly decreased.

In the old days of software boxes, once you opened it, you owned it. Didn't matter if it worked or not.

Developers, marketers, advertisers and businesses should be aware that a smaller reward, when associated to a prized, highly valued item, will help reinforce and validate our feelings about the item.

A larger reward for the same item triggers feelings that it's not the item we're really interested in, but the reward itself and that's where the value is.

In other words, offering a higher reward than what the prized item is worth only leads to feelings that we're being paid to falsely believe in the claimed value of the prized item.

This results in a phenomenon known as "*buyer's remorse*".

Marketers, advertisers, businesses and developers who create strong positive emotional relationships can avoid buyer's remorse (cognitive dissonance), and build long-lasting relationships with an increased likelihood of repeated activities and purchases.

Psychological Factors

Behavioral scientists spend their time exploring and studying the principles and rules of how people respond to their environments.

It's the result of these psychological studies that help us understand how people will react to our software and applications. This understanding is used to measure and influence how people will react and engage.

The benefits of the knowledge provided through Big Data, data mining and predictive behavior analysis are amplified when we apply our knowledge of the basic psychological factors that influence us.

Hierarchy of Human Needs

People are naturally motivated to achieve certain needs.

These needs are sought and accomplished in a specific order. As one hierarchical level is satisfied, the next is sought immediately.

Gamification strategies play off of the Hierarchy of Human Needs. And much like real life, people do not always get to progress from one level to the next without experiencing challenges and failure.

Everyone has the ability and desire to move up from one level to the next. In real life, our ability to move through the levels is blocked by our failure to accomplish lower level needs. Things like life experiences or even the loss of a job can cause us to fluctuate between levels.

Check out Maslow's Hierarchy of Needs on Wikipedia at http://en.wikipedia.org/wiki/Maslow's_hierarchy_of_ needs

The needs are broken in to a 5 level model represented by a simple pyramid.

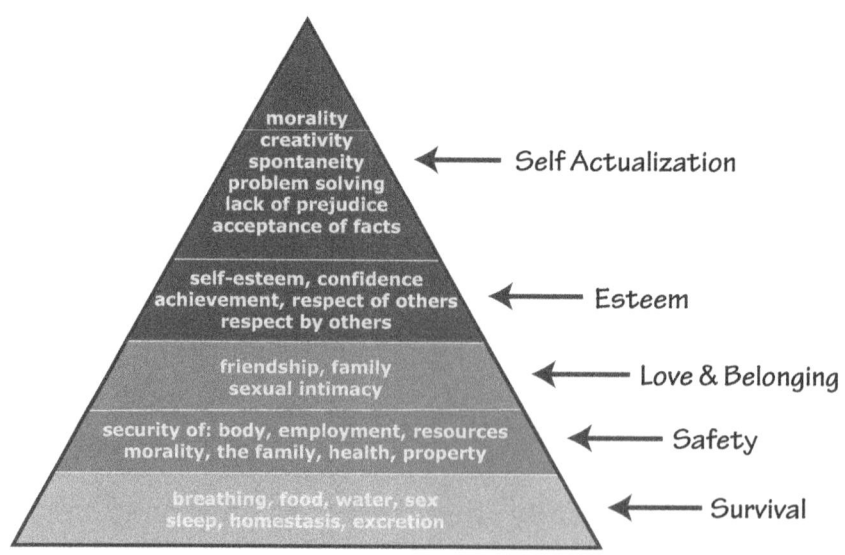

We are motivated by the strong desire to fulfill each need. The longer we are denied a need, the greater our desire to fulfill it.

The lower most needs must be satisfied first before we are able and motivated to accomplish the next level.

The first level of the model begins with **Survival**. Survival includes basic and essential biological and physiological needs such as air, food, drink, shelter, warmth, sex and sleep.

The second level is **Safety**. Safety includes the need for protection from elements, security, order, law, stability, freedom from fear.

The third level is **Love and Belongingness**. Nobody wants to live their lives alone. Love and Belongingness includes friendship, intimacy, affection and love, community groups, family, friends and romantic relationships.

The fourth level is **Esteem**. The needs of our Esteem include achievement, mastery, independence, status, dominance, prestige, self-respect and the respect from others including our peer groups.

The fifth and final level is **Self-Actualization**. Our Self-Actualization needs include realizing our personal potential, self-fulfillment, morality, creativity, personal growth, lack of prejudice and peak experiences.

Reinforcers

There are two behavioral reinforcers that marketers, advertisers, businesses and developers should be aware of in their Gamification strategies.

Primary and Secondary reinforcers.

Primary Reinforcers:

are biological and physiological in nature. Primary reinforcers are rewards that can include food, drink, water, sex, sleep, pleasure and more.

Secondary Reinforcers:

are those that are learned. Secondary reinforcers are rewards that can include money, toys, level-ups, experience points, badges, good grades or scores, and other related things.

Why does Facebook work so well?

 One reason Facebook is so incredibly successful is because it satisfies a great number of our basic hierarchical needs, especially our need for social validation. Social validation is status and acceptance from our social peer groups.

By varying rewards and providing them intermittently, Gamification can create incredibly strong motivators.

Intermittent Reinforcement is a term coined by B.F. Skinner (Wikipedia https://en.wikipedia.org/wiki/B._F._Skinner). Skinner was a scientist specializing in psychology and behavior.

The term describes a reward that is given only part of the time when a *"subject"* gives the desired behavior or response.

Think of a rat running a maze. The rat is motivated to run the maze by receiving a reward at the end.

If the rat receives a reward each and every time it runs the maze, it will quickly become disinterested because it has already fulfilled its desire to survive (the lowest level on our Hierarchy of Needs map).

If the rat is rewarded only part of the time (intermittently), it will run the maze continuously because of its desire to fulfill the need to survive.

Primary Reinforcers are biological and physiological.

Secondary Reinforcers are learned.

Intermittent Reinforcers are given only part of the time.

Motivators

There are two basic psychological Gamification motivators. Extrinsic *(from outside forces)* and Intrinsic *(from internal forces)*.

Extrinsic motivators can include survival, safety, love and belonging.

Intrinsic motivators can include love and belonging, esteem and self-actualization.

The Gamification of real-world activities can create incredibly powerful motivators that drive people to do what you want and need them to do, when you want them to do it.

There are many methods for motivating behaviors with Gamification. Most center around:

Engagement:

Increasing the engagement and interest of the customer by challenging and rewarding them for their continued interactions.

Competition:

Introducing competition within a social community where members compete for status, experience, leadership and more.

Teamwork:

Encouraging customers to work in groups or teams to help other individuals or the community as a whole. Motivation is increased by the desire to contribute and not let other members down.

Progression:

The use of game mechanics that include feedback, badges, levels and leveling to encourage consumers and gamers to work for higher levels of achievement and much larger goals.

Addiction:

The embedding of certain behavioral habits to motivate consumers and gamers to repeat actions and activities as a pre-programmed response.

Combining one or more of these motivators can turn a simple every-day activity into a highly charged Gamification experience.

The most often used mechanic in computer gaming is competition. Players compete against each other, teams of players, or even against the computer itself.

Other motivators include cues such as ranks, levels, badges, progression and status. All of which make for deeper engagement, more frequent and longer game play and long-term loyalty.

Extrinsic Motivators

Creative Commons: www.flickr.com
Jurgen Appelo m30.me/flickr

Extrinsic motivators are related to our need for survival and safety.

Extrinsic motivators are incredibly powerful and the easiest to use, but they are not as long lasting as the forces related to the need for esteem and self-actualization.

The flaw with Extrinsic Motivators is that we only need so much of them before our needs are completely met.

Having more doesn't really help us beyond our basic need.

A hungry person only needs enough food to satisfy the hunger craving. Once the craving is gone, more food has no impact.

It's because of this that extrinsic motivators are short-term and impossible to sustain.

Status is an example of an Extrinsic Motivator. It's an

extremely powerful extrinsic motivator and satisfies our need to feel important and privileged. It even boosts our sense of self-esteem (to a degree).

However, there is only so much status one can have. After a while, rewarding more status becomes counterproductive.

> *The definition of Status within a Gamification context is the position occupied in a given setting. We all occupy several statuses and play roles that may be associated with them. A role is a set of norms, values, behaviors and personality characteristics attached to a status.*
> *(http://www.sparknotes.com/sociology/society-and-culture/section4.html)*

Within a video game, status can be established through the use of points, scores, experience, levels and badges. The higher one's status, the greater their credibility, respect and influence within the social community.

Yahoo Answers uses both levels and points to establish status within their community. The more questions answered and the greater the number of "Best Answer" votes, the higher one's status and social validation within the Yahoo community.

Social media sites make use of Status as an Extrinsic Motivator with great effectiveness.

Facebook and Quora use "*Likes*" and "*Up Votes*" as extrinsic motivators, even though these types of motivators lack any form of tangible value. People feel validated and recognized for their contribution within the community.

Social status within a community works as a very powerful

motivator but is not sustainable and therefore does not work so well as a tool for long-term engagement.

Social Proof is another form of Extrinsic Motivation. It's the sense of approval, belonging, placement and status within a community.

Social Proof is loosely based on the concept that "*birds of a feather flock together, and one bird always leads the flock*".

Almost every pizza-joint in New York city boasts of being New York's BEST PIZZA!

This is a simple form of social proof. The pizza joint brags that their social community has voted them as the best.

By the way, if you make it to New York definitely try the pizza! It doesn't seem to matter who you get it from, it's all pretty amazing.

By J. Howard Miller, via Wikimedia Commons

Intrinsic Motivators

Intrinsic Motivators are those that appeal to our need for belonging, esteem and self-actualization.

When used within the right motivational context, they too can be incredibly powerful drivers. The benefit of Intrinsic Motivators is that they build long-term engagement.

Within the scope of Gamification,

Intrinsic Motivators can include these game mechanics:

Real-Time Feedback:

reinforcing useful behaviors by letting players evaluate and measure their progress

Transparency:

allowing gamers to compare their personal efforts against those within their gaming community

Goal Setting:

providing context and focus to the meanings of all interactions, rewards and behaviors

Competition:

the desire to constantly improve to gain status within the social group

Badges:

symbolic imagery to the player's mastery of the game to other players

Leveling Up:

an opportunity to constantly improve and hone skills, learn more and progress within the game environment

Teams:

the ability to combine efforts as a unified force

Mastery:

> allowing players to begin with a minimal skillset or understanding but to progress through more difficult environments, levels and situations as their skills and knowledge improves

These mechanics give a good broad overview of the how Gamification works mostly from a gamified experience. The psychology that drives Gamification intrinsic motivators is much larger than just that.

The Gamification psychology of intrinsic motivators are based on the Hierarchy of Needs:

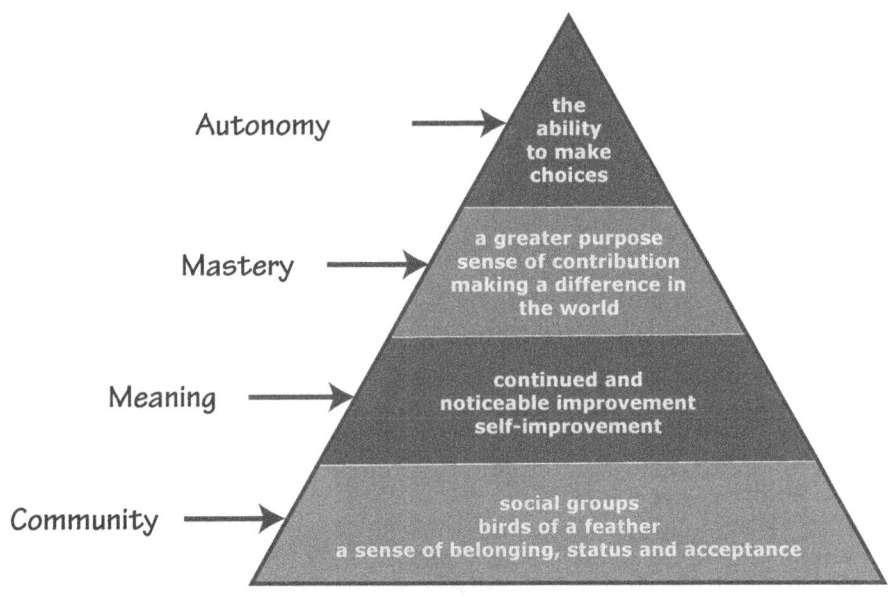

Autonomy → the ability to make choices

Mastery → a greater purpose sense of contribution making a difference in the world

Meaning → continued and noticeable improvement self-improvement

Community → social groups birds of a feather a sense of belonging, status and acceptance

Community:

> The sense of belonging within a social group of like-minded people who share similar values and beliefs. But not only the sense of belonging, the sense of acceptance, validation and status within that community.

Meaning:

The sense of a higher purpose that inspires and moves us towards the greater common good. This is the story that is drives, inspires and provides a sense of contribution that will make a difference.

Mastery:

The measurability of our skills and expertise within the community within the context of the meaning. Mastery is what we've learned, what our experience levels are and a measurement of how much further we have to go in order to achieve the ultimate goal.

Autonomy:

The empowerment and ability to make our own choices. Choices and decisions have an impact on what we do, what we've done and where we'll go next. It is the right to freedom from external controls and influences and gives us a sense of independence and control over our own destiny.

Community

Most people in the world feel lonely at some time in their lives and they don't like it.

When consumers and gamers belonging to a community they feel connected, wanted and validated.

Community appeals to one's sense of Love, Belongingness and Esteem on the Hierarchy of Human Needs. And it is community that gamers and consumers crave the most but feel they lack the most.

The desire for compassion and connection are the most important need after basic survival. But to create a community, the community must be real and genuine to be trusted, desired and valued.

Real and genuine connections come from **quality** (not quantity) interactions. When consumers or gamers feel emotionally connected to their community they are inspired and motivated to contribute, participate and engage with it, and help other members within the community.

It is this innate desire to help that provides the fuel to the community within Gamification.

> *"People are more willing to help than you think, and that can be important to know when you're trying to get the resources you need to get a job done, when you're trying to solicit funds, or what have you."*
> *Frank Flynn – Associate Professor of Organizational Behavior, Stanford GSB*

People really like helping other people. The desire to help primarily driven by the desire to build connections and receive validation. Friends and strangers like us more when we give them the opportunity to help us.

The same stands true when after we fail, we ask for help. Most people are more inclined to help us after we've failed because it gives them an elevated sense of status, which in turn further motivates and engages them.

People who have been asked to help and have given help,

will also be far more inclined to help again.

In fact, someone who has helped you is far more likely to *give you help again* than someone you have helped and *"owes you a favor"*.

The best, most effective, least expensive and easiest help that can ever be given is advice. This is why advice driven websites like YELP! do so well.

By asking for advice, the members of the community feel they are valued, are capable of contributing and their status is psychologically validated.

By giving advice, the members of the community feel a stronger connection to the community along with a greater sense of contribution to the health and welfare of the community.

Meaning

Think of meaning as "your story".

Meaning is the snapshot of the community's beliefs. It's the story that drives and inspires the community and is based on the beliefs and attitudes of the community.

Meaning is the higher purpose, the greater goal that makes every effort seem worthwhile.

Meaning is the reason a gamer or consumer will engage with your activity rather than do something else, even if that something else is to do nothing at all. Doing nothing at all is far easier than anything you could possibly expect of your audience.

Do you remember the story of Jarod* from Subway?

The idea that someone could lose over 240 pounds by eating 700 sub-sandwiches is almost nonsensical, but the achievement was inspiring. The achievement had meaning and purpose that served to inspire a community.

> *For the sake of our example, let's forget about what a terrible and horrible person Jarod turned out to be. However, Jarod's current story serves as an extreme example of Cognitive Dissonance.*

Meaning doesn't need to make logical or realistic sense. However, it does need to be big enough in story, concept and structure to inspire your consumers and gamers to take action.

Your story is just as valid saving the real-world's poor as it is saving a medieval magical land from alien space invaders.

It doesn't matter if you're a marketer, advertiser, business person or an app developer. If your story is strong, inspirational and has a meaningful connection, your audience will be far more inclined to follow it.

Gamified participants want to get busy achieving things. They want to be productive. Productivity comes from meaning and productivity further aids the belief system of the community.

In a Gamified task or activity, the audience wants to receive rewards, achieve goals, progress through new exciting levels, learn more and receive the validation and accolades afforded them from the community. And this is another reason why meaningful goal needs to be present.

Think of it this way...the meaning behind losing weight simply for the sake of just shedding a few pounds because you have nothing better to do with your time is not as strongly and powerfully motivating as losing a few pounds because your very life immediately depends on it.

Filmmakers and storytellers discovered the importance of meaning long ago.

Story is the *most* powerful tool available to marketers, advertisers, businesses and developers for creating meaning.

Creative Commons - Wikipedia Attribution: Rienpost at Dutch Wikipedia

Stories create intense visual pictures and they also create strong relatable connections with the audience.

People relate emotionally and physiologically to stories.

When you watch a movie, you experience what the characters are experiencing. You tense up when the story is tense, you laugh when the story is funny and you cry when the story is sad. People are emotional beings and we relate and feel the emotions of others around us.

Stories do not need to be complicated or complex. However, they do need to have a beginning, middle and an end. This is known as the story "*arc*".

Think of the beginning as the routine, the daily grind or the status quo. The regular grind that all of us goes through every day.

The middle introduces conflict... Cognitive Dissonance!

Cognitive dissonance like conflict, is uncomfortable and commands change. The demand and command for change leads to resolution and a resolution is an ending. Just make it one your participants want.

Yes, it really is that simple.

Because your audience, whether they're gamers, consumers or employees react to stories, your stories have to be personal. The more personal your story, the deeper the emotional attachment. The deeper the emotional attachment the greater the engagement.

Mastery

Mastery is the sense of having accomplished a goal by using knowledge and skills that have improved over time with experience.

Our understanding of the importance of our mastery comes from feedback.

Quantitative feedback is a measurable value such as the points we've scored in a game or the grade we got on an exam.

The higher the number of points or the higher the grade, the greater our sense of mastery.

Qualitative feedback is based on experience. The longer we engage and interact, the more experienced we become the greater our sense of mastery. In video games we represent experience with difficulty levels. The assumption is that the longer you've played the game, the more likely you are to continue by playing at higher levels of difficulty.

Feedback is key and essential to engagement and motivation. Instant feedback within Gamification is expected and must be immediately connected to the event or activity.

The concept Feedback in video games can take many the forms including levels and scores. A level shows the notion of difficulty, achievement and mastery. Each level requires progressively more knowledge and improved skills to master.

Attribution: Wikipedia - ElHeineken

The more your audience is *encouraged* by immediate Feedback, the more motivated and engaged they'll become.

However, if Mastery comes too easily, it will be neither desired or valued by the community.

If Mastery is too difficult, the participants become discouraged and will give up before they can achieve goals.

The difficulty is balancing the *Mastery Proposition* so that it starts simple, almost a tutorial of what the opportunities, activities and rules are all about. As the audience's skills and knowledge improve, each level becomes progressively more difficult, in turn requiring an improvement of skills and knowledge.

Variety is the spice of life. Variety can provide the audience with the chance to experiment and practice those skills in new ways without putting anything they've gained at risk.

Goals tie in to the meaning of the task. The achievement of a goal leads the audience to a greater sense of accomplishment and contribution to the community as a whole.

However, a major goal extended over a long period of engagement can be overwhelming and frustrating for the participant.

Marketers, advertisers, businesses and developers can break major goals down into smaller, easier to accomplish shorter goals. Each smaller goal must be specific and focused within the global context of the major goal in order to avoid confusion. And each of the shorter goals, when added up, equal a major goal.

By breaking major goals into smaller, easier goals... each with their own rewards and feedback mechanisms, participants become much more responsive. Each of the smaller goals must be specific and focused within the context of the larger goals in order to avoid confusion.

Smaller goals are easier to accomplish and they provide feedback and rewards more quickly. This increases the likelihood that your audience will want to participate and remain engaged. Participants are far more likely to complete all of the tasks you've set out for them if there are a number of smaller, easier to accomplish tasks they can work through.

> *Think of dieting. The major goal is to lose 50 pounds within 12 weeks. By itself, this may seem rather overwhelming. The only feedback mechanism is the loss of 50 pounds after 12 weeks.*

> *Instead, if we set a series of smaller goals...4 pounds per week, the individual tasks are far easier to achieve, provide relatively quick feedback and ultimately add up to the loss of 50 pounds within the 12 weeks.*

Progress feedback is an important element of motivation and engagement and smaller goals represent a bigger opportunity to provide feedback that has meaning while implying status within the community.

Adding rewards for accomplishing each activity increases engagement along with the desire to continue.

The use of *multiple* rewards within smaller actionable tasks, also serves to motivate and build stronger engagement. An example would be the use of a quantitative ranking system where the reward is either a level increase or game points. A secondary reward could be experience points or a prized badge.

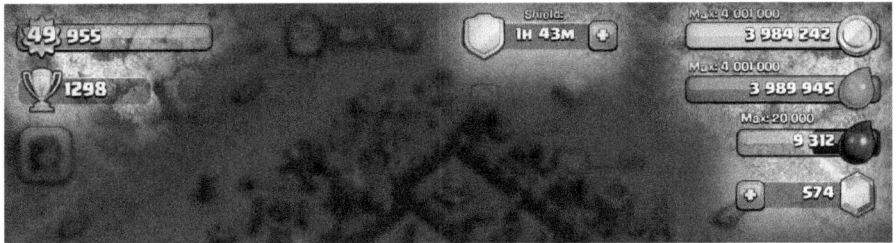

Clash of Clans uses experience levels, experience points, trophies, shields, gold, elixir, dark elixir and diamonds to engage and motivate players

In the mobile game *Clash of Clans*, players are engaged by building villages, attacking villages, accumulating resources and using those resources to continually improve and upgrade their villages. As they do so, they earn experience points, levels, gold, elixir and badges.

Experience points and levels are used within the game to identify the status of the gamer within the community. Experience points and levels are never lost, they are always gained and they encourage the player to be continuously active.

"*Leagues*" are another popular status device used within video gaming.

The more a player engages and plays the game, the more they win tournaments, the more they interact with other players within the community, the *higher* their league status increases.

Failure to login and play, losing tournaments, non-participation and refusing to help other players on their team can result in the loss of game points and league status.

The higher the game points and league status, the greater the participant's perception of their mastery and status of the game, and the higher the community's perception of the participant's mastery and status.

Multiple, overlapping rewards within the smaller and more achievable goals improve the participant's experiences and helps them progress through the activities to mastery. Overlapping multiple rewards removes the linearity of the experience and extinguishes the desire to give up or abandon the activity.

Rules help establish new challenges and goals while influencing creativity and motivation.

An example of rule can be a deadline...a timer that commands the achievement be reached within a specified amount of time. The closer a player gets to the deadline, the harder they work to achieve the goal.

Rules establish boundaries that allow the audience to experience the space in which they're operating and make that space more entertaining and engaging.

Rewards, feedback and rules are not enough on their own though to engage and motivate participants to Mastery.

Participants have to genuinely care and believe in the meaning and purpose behind the activities and goals in order for them to be inspired enough to strive for Mastery. Mastery and Meaning go hand-in-hand:

> *Most people genuinely want to lose weight and truly care about losing the weight. However, feedback and Mastery of weight loss is a very slow process and ... dieting is really hard to do. Making the commitment*

is easy enough, but sticking with the commitment is altogether another matter.

By capitalizing on the desire to lose the weight, by breaking the task into more manageable smaller goals as discussed earlier, the smaller goals become more achievable and the feedback is more rapid. It's much easier to lose 2 pounds twenty times than it is to lose 40 pounds once. Weekly "cheat nights" are stronger rewards, especially if the goals are being achieved, than one big meal at the end of the ultimate goal.

Autonomy

People around the world are the same.

They all want *freedom*.

They want to be heard and they want to know their ideas and opinions are valued and will be validated by their peers.

By contributing and being involved in a community, people feel far more valued, important and emotionally connected. Especially when the community responds. Direct feedback from the community is valued and important because it directly validates the contribution that's been made.

Participants want to be in control of their own creative processes. By providing Autonomy, you allow your participants to create and design their own paths throughout the journey you have planned for them.

Options are choices and creating Autonomy is about providing options. The end goal will always be the same, but the branching opportunities provided by options and choices to arrive at the end goal will be different. Allowing your participants to determine and set their own pathways builds strong intrinsic value.

Options include, but are not limited to "how", "when", "why" and more.

The options you provide have to align with the overall meaning of the ultimate goal, but must also align with the meaning and purpose you've designed for the smaller goals. Options provide Autonomy because they indirectly tell your participants they are being listened to and that their contribution matters.

However, developers, marketers, advertisers and businesses must be careful not to provide too many options, but instead narrow the focus of choices to two or three simple options within context of the goals.

Playful exchanges through chats and other devices within the community help lead to greater sharing and should be encouraged. Sharing will lead to more requests for help from the community, which in turn helps to build the community. This type of jesting builds strong connections between the members of the community.

Jesting and banter demonstrates strength, confidence and warmth. It builds engagement and loyalty, along with a strong sense of a unified community with a distinct personality.

The Laws of Attraction (Wikipedia https://en.wikipedia.org/wiki/Law_of_attraction_(New_Thought)) help define what aspects of personality attract people to other people and apply well within Gamification. There are three basic attraction influencers:

Warmth:

The goodwill we have towards others demonstrates whether the people in authority and power will use their authority and power for our benefit or well-being. A warm person is seen as being caring, benevolent and willing to help the community in positive ways.

Power:

The perception of power comes from one's ability to influence the community and world around them, be it through money, expertise, authority, popularity, status or physical strength.

Presence:

Having presence means having moment-to-moment awareness and being fully present within an interaction. It's about paying attention while interacting with those around you.

Power without warmth creates the fear that the power can be used against you.

Warmth without power implies there is no real ability to provide help.

A lack of presence implies indifference.

Gamification experiences are about community and meaningful choices that lead to Mastery. Autonomy refers to the freedom a person has to make their own choices that lead to Mastery.

Rules and Boundaries for Rewards

Operant Conditions are those that change behaviors through the use of a reinforcement that is given after a desired action.

Our good friend BF Skinner defined three Operant Conditions:

Neutral Operants:

These are responses from the environment that neither increase or decrease the chances of the behavior being repeated.

Reinforcers:

These are responses from the environment that increase the chances of the behavior being repeated.

Punishers:

These are responses from the environment that decrease the chances of the behavior being repeated.

Contingencies are sets of rules that determine and define when a reward will be given out.

When certain conditions are satisfied, rewards can be given to participants, providing the contingencies have been met, to encourage specific behaviors.

Story (Intrinsic Motivator)

People love stories.

Attribution: Wikipedia – Tom Woodward

One of the key components of Gamification is wrapping story around each of the activities and tasks the participant will be engaged in.

Story helps explain and drive the meaning and belief system behind the events and also helps move participants through the experience with a progressive and logical structure.

We discussed story as having a beginning, middle and end.

Story as an *intrinsic motivator* typically consists of three major stages:

Induction:

Induction is similar to an *introduction*. Induction helps participants to learn and understand what the experience is all about, and what the expectations of the participant are.

As the beginning stage of the Gamification experience it introduces the environment, meaning, rule sets, reinforcers, game mechanics, game elements, goals, challenges and of course, the experience itself.
A number of games such as Clash of Clans introduce gamers to the experience by walking them through a guided first-

level, including how to buy and spend in-game currency.

If the Gamification experience involves skills or challenges, the skill required to achieve the first goal should be the lowest possible of the entire experience. Helpful information can be provided at this stage including guided tours and walkthroughs.

The use of these approaches reduces frustration, confusion and abandonment while simultaneously increasing engagement and goal achievements.

The induction stage should be designed to hook participants and completely engage them.

Immersion:

Immersion, as the second stage, is about escalating the experiences through increased difficulty, skills, knowledge, rewards and achievements.

Mastery is about balance. Make the experience too easy, participants become bored. Make the experience too difficult and the participants disengage. An improperly balanced experience is not immersive and results in high rates of drop outs.

Marketers, advertisers, businesses or developers challenge the participant by raising the stakes, ratcheting up the skills and knowledge needed to progress through each level of the experience, and make each level progressively more difficult.

Immersion is about the fun of the journey. A journey is about traveling through the experience, making choices, taking actions, failing and achieving, all with the intention of getting to the end.

Completion:

The ultimate goal of the Gamification experience is successfully completing the experience.

For marketers and advertisers, this could be transitioning a lead through to becoming a customer. For a business it could be improved employee performance. For a video game, it's as simple as winning the game.

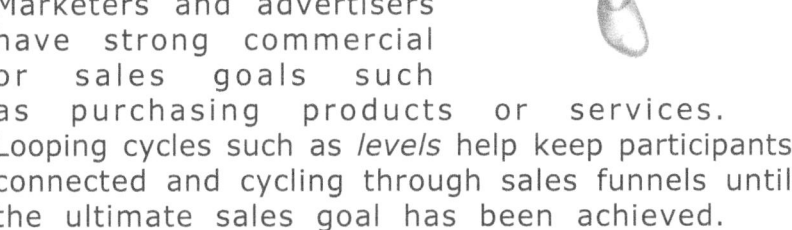

Marketers and advertisers have strong commercial or sales goals such as purchasing products or services. Looping cycles such as *levels* help keep participants connected and cycling through sales funnels until the ultimate sales goal has been achieved.

In linear digital marketing, marketers refer to the concept of a sales funnel where web visitors are funneled towards a desired behavior. Within Gamification marketing, visitors who do not "funnel" are provided with meaning and then re-channeled towards other more engaging behaviors through a variety of autonomous choices and options.

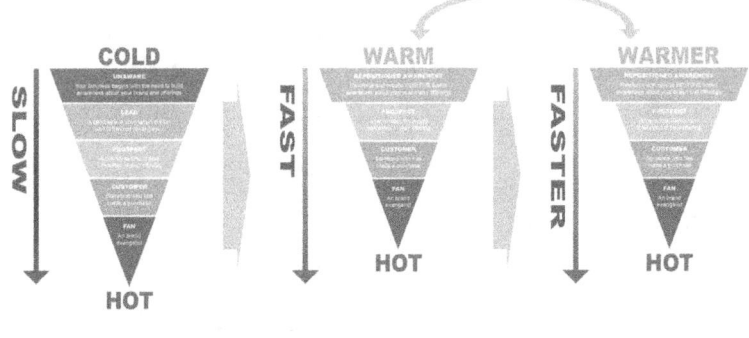

Traditional Sales Funnel   Gamification Sales Funnel

Motivation Driving the Audience

The concept of one-size fits all doesn't fit in the digital world. Participants of your Gamification experience will always be driven by one or more motivators that include:

- The appetite to complete goals couple with the status afforded by the accomplishment.

- The enjoyment of the experience, the thrill of the journey and the satisfaction of curiosity.

- The sense of community and socializing within their peer and community groups.

- The fun of it.

I Expect and Want to Fail

Failure is an option.

It's an important one and it's a good one.

Failure in Gamification is not a label but rather an event or occurrence.

By making failure anything but an event, you make failure a bad thing. Your participants will experience shame, remorse and guilt, and will immediately disengage from the experience.

It's preferred to allow your participants the option to fail.

Failure within the context of the Gamification experience

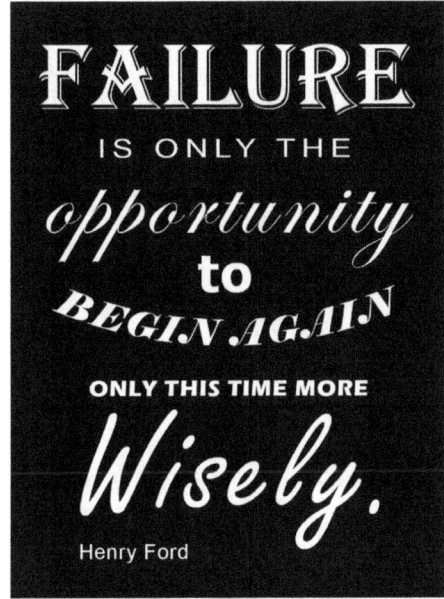

FAILURE IS ONLY THE *opportunity* to BEGIN AGAIN ONLY THIS TIME MORE *Wisely.*

Henry Ford

leads to greater creativity, experimentation and an exploration of options and choices. Experimentation improves the sense of Autonomy and places participants in control.

When people are permitted to fail, they tend to innovate and actually end up succeeding more often because they feel more engaged and in control of the process.

Participants should be encouraged to push the limits of the boundaries of their skills, knowledge and experience without the fear of risk. Pushing limits beyond risk keeps participants highly engaged and powerfully motivated.

Frustration comes from a lack of understanding of a clear rule set. This leads to failure without knowing why. Participants resent experiences that do not provide an explanation of the rules and why and how failure can occur. Therefore, it's incredibly important to ensure there is no failure without awareness.

> *"I have not failed. I've just found 10,000 ways that won't work"*
> *Thomas A. Edison on the Lightbulb*

Engagement

When Gamification is used in marketing, advertising, business or app and game development, participants find the activities more accessible.

Attribution: Wikipedia – Ygor Oliveira

They are more naturally inclined to interact and be engaged. People like fun and will seek out fun activities.

When a participant is successfully engaged in the activity we've designed for them, they will interact more often and for longer. They become more loyal and are more likely to convert and participate in other desired behaviors such as making purchases.

Techniques to Permanent Engagement

If there is no obvious or compelling reason for the audience to engage, then they will not.

To create permanent engagement, marketers, advertisers, businesses and developers need to create *Behavioral Momentum.*

Behavioral Momentum is the tendency to keep doing what you're doing, even when there is no immediate reward.

A high degree of behavioral momentum is sustained from an "avoidance schedule". In the avoidance schedule, participants continuously engage so as to avoid negative motivators or consequences.

A negative consequence could be the loss of a badge as the result of not having logged in for a certain period of time.

Some video games encourage behavioral momentum and permanent regular engagement by offering daily, weekly and monthly rewards for playing every day.

Abandonment (Avoiding It)

Marketers, advertisers, businesses and developers need to consider that their audience has many activities to choose from in their daily lives. Inaction, that is doing nothing at all, is also a choice they have. Many of these things can be far more interesting to them than the desired behaviors and actions you would like them to take.

When implementing a Gamification plan, the activities, tasks and desired behaviors have to be weighed and measured against what our audience would prefer to do. The balance has to be greater to engage than to disengage.

Delaying reward or feedback can also result in demotivating participants. If a reward is going to be delayed and the participant is aware of the delay, the participant is quite likely to choose something else to do with their time instead.

To avoid abandonment, design and layer multiple activities and rewards within smaller sections and smaller goal based activities. This is a form of redirection and it increases motivation and engagement by distracting the participant from the main, delayed activity.

Gamification Mechanics

Motivational Behaviors, Mechanics and Devices

Gamification is accomplished by applying game mechanics and game design practices to non-game activities. This technique has proven to exponentially multiply conversions and purchases.

Core to an immersive approach, certain elements are required to turn visitors to participants.

Achievements:

Game developers have used a variety of symbols to show the accomplishment of a task.

In real-life, people are rewarded with medals, crowns, money, increased status, special favors, wreaths, laurels and other desired objects. In the digital realm, we use similar symbols including badges, points, scores, trophies and levels.

Almost every digital community uses some form of symbolic reward for participation and engagement. The most common symbol of achievement is a badge.

Badges work because of basic, logical factors:

Goal Setting:

Badges serve as an indicator of accomplishment. They encourage further engagement and challenge participants to work harder to achieve higher goals. Goal setting plays well when the goal is a slightly more difficult than the participant's current skill, and feedback is given right away.

Direction:

Badges are symbolic of achievements in context of the rules and boundaries. Rules and boundaries direct participants towards expected behaviors and the badges serve as rewards for having fulfilled those behaviors.

Trustworthiness:

Badges are a strong visual indicator of the participant's expertise, commitment, reputation, activeness and trustworthiness within the community.

Status:

Badges are a symbol of status that validate the participant's social standing within the community and boast of achievements and accomplishments. Participants are highly driven for status and social validation within their communities.

Community:

Badges unify communities and teams of players, identify shared experiences and encourage further participation.

Achievements are Extrinsic Motivators. Achievements on their own are only one layer of what people care about within the Gamification loop.

Appointments:

Appointments are quite literally just that, specific times and places a participant must be.

Behavioral Momentum:

Behavioral Momentum is the inclination to keep repeating a given activity.

Cascading Information Theory:

Cascading Information Theory states that information should be released slowly and in small pieces in order to avoid overwhelming participants.

Community Collaboration:

Community Collaboration brings participants together to solve problems. Participants are highly motivated to live up to the expectations of their communities and to help improve the health of the community. Community Collaboration motivators should be much stronger than competitive motivators.

Countdowns:

Countdowns are timers. Timers are used as a pressure cooker to encourage participants to perform tasks at a high level of efficiency and quickly.

Discovery:

Discovery allows participants to explore and discover new and exciting things. It plays off of a person's natural sense of curiosity. The element of surprise can serve to further engage players and encourage exploration. Discovery is a powerful motivator because it is an Intrinsic Motivator.

Free Lunch:

Everyone loves getting something for free, especially when someone else has done all the hard work for them.

Infinite Gameplay:

Infinite Gameplay is gameplay which has no known end. These are games that are in a constant state of play. These types of games are incredibly powerful tools for marketers and advertisers who want to capture more hot leads within their sales funnels.

Levels:

Levels are systems of ramps where participants receive feedback based on their experience, amount of play, achievements and points. As participants progress through higher levels, their skills are further challenged. Leveling is one of the highest motivational factors. There are three types of leveling ramps:

- Flat: the level progression difficulty increases at a steady, linear rate

- Exponential: the level progression difficulty increases more and more with each level

- Wave Function: the level progression difficulty can increase and decrease as the participants progress through to higher levels

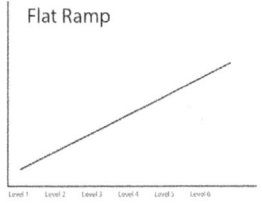

Flat Ramp

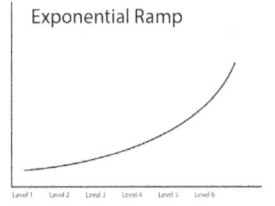

Exponential Ramp

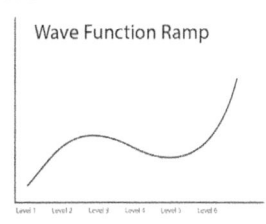

Wave Function Ramp

Loss Aversion:

Loss Aversion is the desire to avoid negative consequences. In a great many games, the negative consequences, or loss, for irregular and or inconsistent participation can be a loss of progress or awards.

Lottery:

Lottery determines the final winner based on chance. As a motivator, Lottery has a strong initial motivation but quickly annoys participants and leads to abandonment.

Ownership:

Ownership is another word for Autonomy. This is a sense of control through the ability to make decisions based on a variety of options and choices. Care must be taken to ensure not too many choices or options are provided, and the choices that are offered must have direct significance to the goals and outcomes desired and must be in context to the meaning.

Meaning:

Meaning is the sense of doing something that has great significance and importance. It serves as a belief system that can powerfully inspire and influence participants to take actions. Meaning also comes from creating an environment that doesn't yet exist and then applying a skill to that environment.

Points:

Points are a quantitative feedback mechanism given for actions. They are a form of achievement and indicators of progress. Virtual currencies are a form of points.

Quests:

Quests are usually time limited or limited to competition. A quest is a journey where participants must overcome a variety of obstacles and challenges. Quests must be of the right level of challenge and provide clear goals and feedback. The goals of a quest can inspire strong emotional connections within a community.

Reward Schedules:

Reward Schedules are timed reward delivery systems.

Urgency:

Urgency is an extreme form of self-motivation. Urgency is the desire to act immediately combined with the hope there will be success.

Virality:

Virality requires multiple people to engage and participate, but to also encourage the participation of others within their social groups.

From Activity to Engagement

Although game elements, mechanics and design are relatively easy to implement to non-gaming activities, the true differentiator between an activity that has game-like elements and an actual Gamification experience is the autonomy to make choices that control the outcomes, and the feedback mechanisms that indicate accomplishment.

Merely *presenting* information through Gamification

experiences is not true engagement. Participants must not only be provided choices and options within the experience itself, but also in the possible paths to purchase and consumption along with the reward for purchases and consumption. Most often, this is presented in the form of couponing for deeper discounts on desired items on the next purchase.

Fun

A truly engaging Gamification experience is fun.

People are not usually inclined to engage in an activity simply for the sake of the activity. Instead, they engage in activities that are fun and entertaining.

Fun experiences are physiological and release highly addictive *dopamine* to the brain. Examples of fun activities include:

Problem Solving

Problem solving is an Intrinsic Motivator that plays off the natural need to solve problems. By presenting problems in a manner that allows for creativity, compensates for failure, allows innovation, and provides systems of rewards, greater participation and engagement can be expected.

Collaboration

People enjoy sharing their skills and expertise while collaborating with teams to overcome obstacles. Collaboration is a form of community contribution and leads to social validation and status.

Exploration

Providing a choice of paths within environments engages participants to explore and discover what the environment has to offer. Choices and options encourage creativity and innovation, which in turn lead to greater engagement and participation.

Building

People like to build and collect things. They are naturally motivated to complete their collections by collecting all the possible elements that add up to make a collection. Badges, levels, achievements, status are all forms of collectibles that can be used to increase engagement and improve participation and loyalty.

Rewards

People are naturally inclined and hardwired to respond to systems of rewards. When participants in a task, activity or event are rewarded for their participation, they are more likely to complete the task.

Tangible rewards are those that are not virtual or conceptual and include such things as discounts on products and services, free items and so on. We refer to these as *real-world benefits*. ***Real-world rewards*** are extremely powerful motivators.

Intangible rewards are those that are conceptual or virtual. Intangibles include unlockable features, badges, points, levels and experience rewards. Intangibles work incredible well as motivators but their power can be amplified when they are rolled in to the Gamification model. We refer to these as *virtual (in-game) benefits*.

Real-World Benefits versus Virtual (In-Game) Benefits

Marketers, businesses and advertisers use real-world benefits to increase sales, boost revenues or share information across their teams and customers.

They may even use real-world benefits to increase website and social networking activities by offering special discounts or coupons for visits, likes or other engagements.

The first major step towards creating a Gamification model is to identify the real-world objectives and then compare them to the desired Gamification experience.

Once identified, it's then a simple matter of determining the choices and options that should be presented to the participants and the rewards that will be offered for the accomplishments and achievements.

Questions to ask are: Should the Gamification experience include both real-world and virtual rewards? What rewards are highly desired and prized by participants? Can the real-world rewards be properly balanced with virtual rewards to motivate and inspire participants to take action and engage in the experience?

By aligning the choices and options with achievements, taking in to consideration the game design and game mechanics, and contrasting them against how hard the activities or tasks are, marketers, advertisers, businesses and developers can create rewards that are desired and feel right.

The risk is that unnecessarily complex reward systems with many branching mechanisms such as points, leaderboards, rules, stories, levels, experiences, badges and other elements may far exceed and complicate what's required of the experience and result in disengaging the participants.

Rewards for The Sake of Rewards

Rewards offered simply for the sake of the reward itself will not work.

These types of rewards are most often seen in gambling games and generally encourage an initial burst of interest, but that interest very quickly wanes. These types of rewards are not able to keep the participants engaged or motivated.

Simply adding game elements without meaning or context will result in rapid abandonment. Badges, points, experience points, levels, leaderboards have to have meaning and context. Without meaning and context the rewards become monotonous and boring.

Developers will often take the easy way out by offering many rewards with great frequency. The problem with this tactic is that it rarely results in increased engagement and usually gives the impression that the tasks or activities were not worth the value of the reward.

Many business owners and marketers have learned that by frequently and significantly reducing the price of a highly valued product or service, the initial perceived value rapidly decreases.

Buying immediate motivation and engagement exponentially reduces long-term motivation and engagement.

Value of The Rewards

The value of rewards is relative.

Contrary to what one might expect, the smaller the reward and the harder one has to work for the reward, even when the reward is associated to a highly desired item, the greater the reinforcement and validation of the perceived value.

A disproportionately larger reward for the same valued item will subconsciously trigger us to believing the value is only in the *reward itself* and we were mistaken in our perception of the value of the item.

Additionally, the value of the most current reward is always measured against the value of the most previous reward.

If the current reward's value is not significantly greater than the previous reward's value, the participant will feel cheated and frustrated. Participants will feel as though they are being punished.

Violation of expectations is generally seen as aggressive and unfair.

The value of rewards is maintained by avoiding large changes in the structures, rates and values of the rewards.

Rewards Frequency

Events, activities and tasks within Gamification experiences can be rewarded when certain conditions have been met, even at intervals. Rewards and bonuses can be given to encourage behavior by making use of intermittent reinforcements.

An *intermittent reinforcement* is one where each time a desired behavior is achieved, it's not always rewarded, but rather is rewarded occasionally.

There are four types of intermittent reinforcers:

Fixed Interval:

Fixed intervals are scheduled reinforcers that happen whenever the desired behavior occurs, but only after a specific set period of time. An example is a bi-monthly paycheck.

Fixed interval reinforcers are not strong and can lead to abandonment.

Participants will typically reduce or pause their activities after a reward has been given. This reduction of engagement and interaction also disrupts and reduces the participant's motivation to interact and engage.

Unlike Fixed Ratios, there is no sudden bursts of activity as a reward time approaches and instead there is a gradual increase of activity.

Fixed Ratio:

Fixed Ratios apply the reinforcer after a determined number of occurrences of the desired behavior. A sales commission would be based on the number of units sold.

Fixed Ratio reinforcers do not provide consistent, long-term behavioral changes.

Fixed ratios are used to produce predictable patterns of activity. An example would be general activity for a period of time, followed by a sudden burst of rapid activity when the possibility of a reward exists. Activity increases when the likelihood of a reward being provide more quickly becomes present.

Having long periods of time in between intervals of high activity do not provide opportunities to incentivize interaction and engagement.

In fixed ratio applications, marketers, advertisers, businesses and developers need to make use of these long periods of inactivity with incentives for participants to explore and discover the environment, create and innovate, and explore the various features, aspects and challenges the activity will offer.

Variable Intervals:

Variable Intervals are used when the desired behaviors are reinforced after varying periods of time. An example would be job promotions or special recognitions.

Variable Interval reinforcers are incredibly strong and resistant to abandonment.

Variable Intervals randomly change the period of time for the next reward after a current reward has been given. Variable Interval schedules produce steady and continuous engagement and interaction activity, but at a slower pace.

Much like the Variable Ratio, there is always a reason for the participant to be engaged and interacting.

Variable Ratio:

Variable Ratio reinforcers apply the reinforcer after a number of desired behaviors have occurred, with the number changing from situation to situation. An example would be a slot machine in which a different and unknown number of desired behaviors such as putting in quarters and pulling the arm are required before a jackpot is rewarded.

Variable Ratio reinforcers consistently produce desired behavioral changes that are highly resistant to abandonment.

Variable ratios induce participants to engage and interact steadily and with higher frequency. The frequency of sudden bursts of activities will be much lower than that in fixed ratios, but the activities will be more consistent.

A reward can be issued immediately, or a reward can be given hours later. The participant's motivation to interact and engage with the experience is controlled to be spread out over time. Active interactions are lower in a variable ratio because there is no dependence on engagement. Regardless of how fast or how many times the participant seeks out the reward, the reward will not be given any faster.

Variable ratios offer the highest and most consistent engagement and interaction activity.

Each condition is a factor of time, activity and reward. Conditions can be implemented and combined in many different ways to produce desired behaviors.

The Variable Ratio schedule provides the highest opportunity for Gamification success. It creates and maintains high, consistent rates of engagement.

Each engagement has a chance of a reward and interactions are a function of how frequently the participant can expect the reward to happen. The higher the participant's confidence that a reward will be given, the greater their engagement and participation.

Reward Elements and Mechanics

Gamification is the application of game mechanics, theory and design to make non-gaming tasks fun.

There are traditional game elements that are expected and crucial to the success of any Gamification model.

Gamification requires consistency in presentation, flow and dynamics. Participants have learned to expect consistent visual cues and game elements to better understand the rules and boundaries of the Gamification experience.

To complete the Gamification experience, common game reward elements are required. They can be used individually or in any combination you can imagine, providing they work within the context of the meaning of the experience.

Points:

Everyone understands the concept of points and point scoring. Participants are awarded points based on a number of engagement factors including the completion of activities, making purchases, commenting on social networks and so on. A Gamification designer must weigh out the value of desired behaviors and determine the number of points that will be given for each. Points

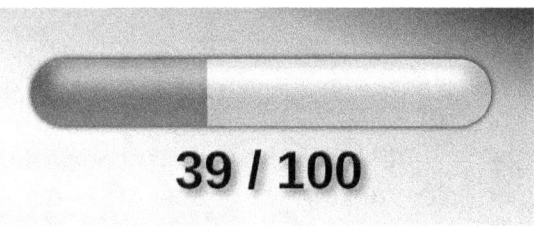

must have context if they are to be prized and if long-term motivation and engagement is to be achieved.

Badges:

Badges, avatars and other related icons have become a new form of engagement currency. Participants are strongly motivated to collect them and badges represent and symbolize achievement and validations. Badges need

to be earned through an ever increasing ramp of difficulty and improved skillsets in order to retain any form of strong meaning within the community.

Good design implementation means creating certain badges that are rare and incredibly difficult to achieve (higher status), and creating mechanisms that allow participants to display all of the badges they have earned over the lifetime of their engagement.

Engagement and interaction can be increased by showing participants the badges they have not yet collected and providing a feedback mechanism that lets them see and understand what actions need to be taken to get them.

Levels:

Levels are a method of segmenting the overall Gamification experience into "bite sized chunks". Each level comes with its own sets of rewards that require varying degrees of knowledge or skills.

Gamification designers typically increase the difficulty of the challenges as participants move from one level to the next.

By exploiting the participant's desire to explore and conquer, levels can also be designed to provide objects, content and information that must be collected before the participant can progress higher.

Unlocks:

People play games for the enjoyment and fun of it. Sometimes the reward for playing is simply the enjoyment of the game.

Unlocks are perks that can be awarded or won that enhance the Gamification experience. Unlocks can include tools or items that improve skills and abilities, prizes, virtual rewards, levels, secret rooms or areas, intangible items or even tangible real-world items.

Participants work to solve puzzles, answer quizzes, conquer or win levels, achieve points or any other type of activity and the reward is an item than is "unlocked" and made available for the participant's use.

Some video games make use of time or limited unlocks. These are items that are unlocked for a short period of time or limited use. Time unlocks can greatly increase engagement as they command the participant to engage in specific activities with a sense of urgency.

Collectables:

Collecting and collection building is an important and powerful tool in Gamification.

Participants enjoy building items or collecting items and are driven to complete their collections.

A strong motivator to pushing a participant to collecting is to either give them one or two collectable elements immediately, or to award the collectable items as low-level and easy to accomplish prizes. Many Gamification experiences will award at least one collectible the moment a participant joins the experience.

Much like with badges, by showing a participant the collectable items they do not have yet and providing feedback on how those items can be acquired, participants become much more engaged and active within the experience.

Load balancing is a factor to consider with Collectibles. Make the collection too large, make the collection too hard or complex, don't provide enough information about the value of the collection and participants will disengage. Make the collection too small or easy and participants will get bored.

Leaderboard:

Leaderboards are ranking systems. They are scoreboards and work by comparing the scores of one participant against another. It's a very simple method of Gamification that helps inspire competition even when the participants are not directly competing against one another or being rewarded for their position on the scoreboard.

Leaderboards are an excellent Gamification tool that can be used by marketers, advertisers, businesses and developers to incentivize interaction and engagement, but without having to pay for it. Leaderboards work especially well when combined with other game reward elements.

Avatars:

Avatars let participants know they are involved and where they stand within the Gamification experience. Avatars are much more than just cute cartoony representations of a player or player's personality.

By applying the concepts of leveling and unlocking, Avatars can be upgraded, modified and otherwise improved to indicate a participant's accomplishments and status within the community.

Avatars, when implemented correctly, can transcend the Gamification environment to social networks, websites, mobile devices and even cellular phones. They can serve to be the perfect viral tool for marketers, advertisers, businesses and developers.

Maps/Boards:

Maps and game boards provide excellent feedback to participants that indicate where they've begun and where they need to go. Game boards are an opportunity to provide reference points for pathing and journeys, and a method of presenting key and essential information.

Virtual pins can be used on a map or game board to stake claims or initiate challenges amongst teams and other players.

Positions on maps or boards can also be used to visually represent progress and accomplishment, much like the concept of a progress bar.

Narratives:

Narrative is the conveyance of story and information and is an important component of Gamification.

Narrative gives participants a greater and more immediate understanding of the meaning of the activities, the purpose, goals and paths they should take. Narrative provides immediate context.

Using Negative Motivators

The concept of Extinction and Abandonment is the result of not providing rewards, not provide the right rewards, or not providing the right rewards at the right time to the participant.

In a ratio schedule, participants will continuously engage for long periods before giving up. In a fixed schedule, participants will increase their engagement as a reward is about to be given and then sharply decrease their engagement or even cease altogether shortly after.

Participants expect sensibility, predictability and consistency. When the do not receive these, their frustration and anger increases and they will abandon the activity.

Behavioral Contrast is a negative motivator. Desired rewards are given each time a desired behavior occurs, or on a ratio schedule. However, after a given interval the next reward is of less value than the previous or is not a desired reward. The participant will meet the reward with frustration and anger.

A reduction in the value of the reward in too sharp a contrast is punishing and negative.

In competitive Gamification team or group environments negative motivators can be powerful incentives for activity and engagement where losing results in actual loss. Participants play harder to win.

Applying Concepts and Making a Gamification Plan

Understanding Your Objectives

There are many methods you can use to implement a Gamification plan into your marketing, advertising, business or development work-flows.

It begins by understanding and knowing what behaviors you would like to encourage from your audience.

Any behavior that provides the results you are looking for is acceptable. This can be anything including social networking, uploading messages or files, downloading coupons, making a purchase, recommendations, giving advice ... anything.

Make a list of all of the tasks and activities you would like to use to motivate behavior and then make a list on how each of those tasks can be made more fun.

If a participant accumulates points, progresses through goals, accomplishes tasks and succeeds with their achievements, what type of rewards are you willing to offer?

Now take in to consideration the various Gamification elements you've listed and decide which are most appropriate within the context of the activities, achievements and goals you've designed. Perhaps your participants begin with badges and then progress to more complex mechanics.

Build Engagement

Community:

What can you build that creates a strong sense of community, that is joyful and playful, authentic, genuine, and allows the members of the community to interact and engage with the Gamification experience while connecting and interacting with other members of the community.

Identify how each element motivates your participants. Does the community appeal to emotion, intellect or perhaps the environmental path...or maybe a combination?

Meaning:

What's your story? What is it that you've designed that will inspire a sense of awe with your participants? Have you created a mythology and if so, how do you expect your participants will connect with the story?

Tell your story from beginning, middle and end. How does Induction, Immersion and Completion fit with your story picture?

Identify how each element of your story serves to motivate participants. Will they connect on an emotional, intellectual or environmental level, or perhaps a combination?

Mastery:

What are the feedback mechanisms you're planning on using? What about the smaller goals, rules, boundaries, major goals, rewards, multiple goals and multiple rewards? How does each mechanism connect to the context of your story, how do they connect with the community and how do they inspire and motivate your participants?

Identify how each element of your feedback mechanism serves to motivate participants. Will your participants connect with each mechanism on an emotional, intellectual or environmental level, or a combination?

Autonomy:

What can you do to provide your participants with autonomy? Will you be creating mechanisms that allow them to be themselves, contribute to the community, allow them to fail, innovate and create?

What mechanisms will you use to allow them to improve their status within the community? Will their status be in flux, shifting up or down based on action or inaction?

What mechanisms will you use to allow the Gamification experience to listen and provide feedback?

Identify how each element and mechanism serves to motivate participants. Will your participants connect on an emotional, intellectual or environmental level, or a combination?

Carefully review your lists. You might find it's far too extensive or that certain elements are not appropriate to the Gamification experience you're designing.

Putting The Plan to Work

Start Small:

It's best to start small and not make the Gamification experience too encompassing.

You can always add elements and improvements as you go along.

Marketers and advertisers are familiar with the concept of A/B testing where they compare one campaign against another. Gamification is not much different. Start with simple elements like progress bars and badges, and then add more elements and features as you receive feedback from your participants.

The Cascading Information Theory tells us to dole out small pieces of information slowly. This is an excellent approach for first venturing in to Gamification.

Testing:

Any developer will tell you that testing is the most integral part of the development process. Testing Gamification is not just about functionality, it helps answer critical questions such as whether the overall experience actually is fun and whether the desired behaviors are taking place and leading to the results you expect.

Testing also identifies whether the Gamification experience is actually engaging for the audience. You may have done everything right, but if the audience won't engage with it, it's not going to work. Testing also allows you to determine if your audience is responding to the incentives you're providing.

Motivators:

Analyze the motivators you've employed.
Is the Gamification experience heavily dependent on Extrinsic motivators? Probably not a good idea if you want to build strong engagement experiences.
Are your participants Intrinsically motivated? If not, it may be time to update with a more balanced motivational experience.

Rinse/Repeat:

Successful Gamification experiences do not attempt large-scale deployments right away. They start small, test concepts and participants, update accordingly, add scalable features and elements and repeat the process larger the next time around.

3 Examples of Gamification Used in Marketing

There are many examples of Gamification in marketing. These are three we've chosen.

Starbucks My Rewards

Starbucks' goal was to increase and improve positive brand recognition, make the Starbucks experience better and increase product sales.

Customers download an application to their mobile device. The application is called My Rewards. Customers are rewarded with a free product for registering the app. Starbucks receives the customer's name, email, age, location and buying habits.

Each time a customer makes a purchase, they are rewarded with stars. The stars add up to free coffees.

Starbucks also uses levels and customers are rewarded for the consistent loyalty. The more often a customer visits a location and makes a purchase, the higher the level they achieve.

Awards include birthday gifts, free coffees and other product offerings.
The end result has been over 5 million engaged customers accounting for over $3.5 billion dollars in sales.

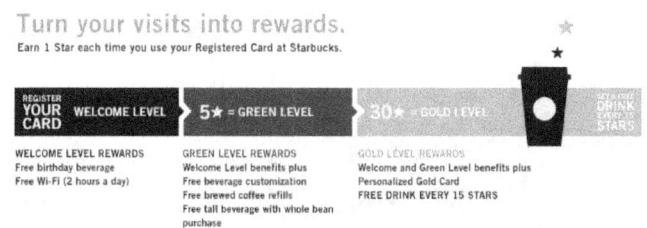

Heineken Star Player

Heineken made use of their soccer Champions League sponsorship to engage sports fans with the goal of increases their product awareness.

Soccer fans download the Heineken app and while they are watching Champions League games on TV are asked to "predict the future" by answer sets of questions.

Questions include "will the penalty be saved", "will the goal be made", "will they score in X seconds".

Points are awarded to participants for correct answers and when there are no games to watch, players can interact with the app by answering trivia questions.

M&M's Eye-Spy Pretzel

M&M's candy wanted to boost their brand awareness and increase social media activities.

They devised a simple online social game that consisted of a full page graphic of row upon row of perfectly aligned M&M candies. Amongst the candy was one, single, lonely pretzel, which participants had to find and report.

The game resulted in a massive brand awareness boost with more than 25,000 likes on Facebook and over 10,000 comments.

3 Examples of Gamification Used in Business

Giff Gaff Magical Gamification

Giff Gaff decided to take a community approach to their Gamification campaign.

They decided to encourage the community of customers to promote each and every service offered by the company, from sales through to support.

When a community member sells a SIM card or provides support to another member, they receive points. Points are converted to cash that can be withdrawn, converted or donated to charity.

BlueWolf

Bluewolf applied Gamification to different areas of employee activity to promote internal collaboration. The goal was to make staff more social.

The company inspired employees to share knowledge through gamified activities by giving out points and rewards to each employee who attempted internal and external collaboration. If employees shared knowledge on LinkedIn and Twitter, they received even more points.

The end result was greatly improved employee productivity, knowledge share and both internal and external collaboration.

The US Army

The US Army employed a Gamification tactic to improve awareness and increase recruitment.

Interested Army candidates downloaded a game for free and then tested their skills in a massive multi-player environment to see if they were soldier material.

Candidates were required to fill out an application with their real information, after which they could join an online community called The Online Army. Skilled players were rewarded with Badges of Honor that replicated actual awards given out in the Army.

Facilities, Providers and Resources

Disrupted Logic: http://www.disruptedlogic.com

Disrupted Logic is a technology development company specializing in Mobile, Big Data, Cognitive Computing and Predictive Behavior Analysis.

ctalyst™: http://www.ctalyst.com

ctalyst™ is the world's most advanced advertising network and technology platform that makes it easy for advertisers to reach a growing mobile market and mobile content publishers to realize new streams of revenue by leveraging technology, social platforms and Gamification engagement.

Badgeville: http://www.badgeville.com

Badgeville offers an enterprise-wide business gamification solution that combines award-winning products and industry-leading expertise.

Bunchball: http://www.bunchball.com

Bunchball launched the gamification industry and generates lasting ROI with real business value by motivating people through big data.

GetSocial: http://www.getsocial.io

Leverage data from sharing buttons and dark social channels to better understand which are the most viral stories to promote on social media.

facebook.com/DisruptedLogic
twitter.com/DisruptedLogic
linkedin.com/company/disrupted-logic-interactive-inc-
youtube.com/user/DisruptedLogic

Disrupted Logic Interactive Inc.

1-206-414-6224

www.disruptedlogic.com
www.ctalyst.com

www.ingramcontent.com/pod-product-compliance
Lightning Source LLC
Chambersburg PA
CBHW070329190526
45169CB00005B/1812